FROM ENSIGN'S TO COLONEL'S STARS

Making Quilts to Honor Those Who Serve

Renelda Peldunas-Harter, COL, USAR, Ret.

Schiffer Publishing Ltd

4880 Lower Valley Road • Atglen, PA 19310

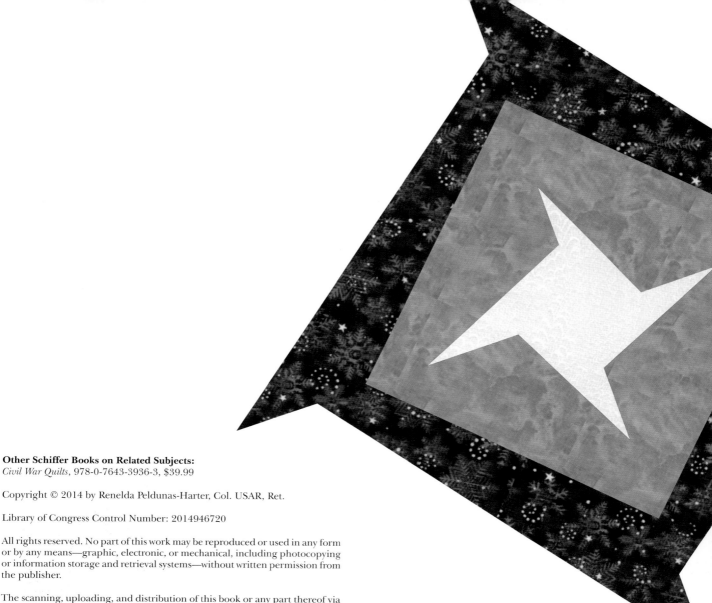

Designed by Molly Shields
Type set in Farnham Display/NewBskvll BT

ISBN: 978-0-7643-4719-1
Printed in China

Published by Schiffer Publishing, Ltd.
4880 Lower Valley Road
Atglen, PA 19310
Phone: (610) 593-1777; Fax: (610) 593-2002
E-mail: Info@schifferbooks.com

For our complete selection of fine books on this and related subjects, please visit our website at www.schifferbooks.com. You may also write for a free catalog.

This book may be purchased from the publisher. Please try your bookstore first.

We are always looking for people to write books on new and related subjects. If you have an idea for a book, please contact us at proposals@schifferbooks.com.

Schiffer Publishing's titles are available at special discounts for bulk purchases for sales promotions or premiums. Special editions, including personalized covers, corporate imprints, and excerpts can be created in large quantities for special needs. For more information, contact the publisher.

Disclaimer: This book contains my recollections of past events. My hope is that I remembered events accurately. Any inaccuracies are my fault and do not reflect upon anyone else.

For Chapter 8, "Military Ranks": American Army Officer Ranks Insignia Icons © Krisdog. *Courtesy of www. bigstockphoto.com*.

DEDICATION

Those of us who serve in the armed forces of the United States stand on the shoulders of the men and women who have served before us; to them I dedicate this book. I have numerous uncles and cousins, as well as other relatives, who have served. I want to specifically mention those in my immediate family:

PRIVATE JOANNES "JOHN" PELDUNAS, USA (WWI)
AG1 ANTHONY P. PELDUNAS SR., USN (WWII, KOREA)
SGT LYLE N. HARTER, USA (WWII)
LTC WILLIAM E. HARTER, USA (RET.) (COLD WAR)
LCDR KENNETH P. PELDUNAS, USN (RET.) (COLD WAR)

CONTENTS

ACKNOWLEDGMENTS

To the veterans who contributed to this book, a special thank you for the quilts and your service! To all the women who contributed their quilts to this book, I would like to thank each of you.

• To Leslie Heilman, for doing *A Major Quilt* and for being a great quilting and knitting friend! Thanks for all the encouragement over the years, especially the ten-year Waterford quilt saga.

• To Carolyn Perry Goins (www.cpgdesigns.com), for all the support and brain-storming sessions. You are a fellow Quilt Market trooper and great friend. Thank you for always being ready to share your love and knowledge of quilting, and thank you for quilting most of my quilts for this book.

• To Catherine Snyder, who started her two quilts somewhere in the Middle East and had them hand-delivered through secret channels via the dark recesses of the Pentagon (and who somehow got them returned through the same channels).

• To Dolores Goodson (www.deeroodesigns. blogspot.com), who volunteered to do any quilt I needed and "Pinked" my platoon.

• To Carol Cushman Casey, who blew me away with the creativity, detail, and story behind her quilt.

• To Linda Burke, who stepped up and turned a red and blue quilt into a Hokie orange and burgundy quilt — go Virginia Tech!

• To Pat Peters, who is the queen of the "math-behind-the-quilt" and enjoys explaining the math behind any quilt! A veteran of the Women's Army Corps (WAC) Army Nurse Corps — thank you for your service.

• To Ann Marie Chaney, a definite Engineer Corps member who is still serving her country today — thank you for the quilt and your service.

• To Didi Salvatierra (www.DidiQuilts.com), whom I've known most of my quilting life — thanks for making a fun quilt.

• To Cindy Sisler Simms (www.CindySimms.net), another quilting buddy who can rub two pieces of fabric together, throw in some imagination, and come up with incredible quilts time and time again. A veteran of the Women's Army Corps, thank you for your service.

• To Elizabeth Frederick Peldunas and Brian Peldunas, who volunteered to scour through my text in search of spelling and grammatical errors; your search paid off — thank you!

• To my husband, Bill, and our sons, Chris and Kevin, for supporting me through my military and quilting careers. Thanks for all the graphics support!

INTRODUCTION

Yes, I know the title should read from Ensign's Bars to Colonel's Eagles, but that didn't sound as sexy as Colonel's Stars! Everyone knows that what colonels really want are stars, not just eagles! Enough about ambition, though, and more about quilting!

Quilts tell a story and what better way to tell the story of our service members than through quilts. Quilts are inspired by many factors and mean different things to different people. Back in the day, quilts were instruments of necessity, to provide warmth, to recycle old blankets, and to use up scraps of precious fabrics. Today, quilts are still made out of necessity, but they are much more. They are objects of art and they can be a cathartic experience. They can exorcize guilt, celebrate life's milestones, and they can commemorate happy and sad events.

My family has always been proud of our service in the military, starting with my immigrant grandfather. He could not speak English very well, but that did not hinder his pride in serving during World War I. During World War II, my father, his brothers, and my father-in-law all served our country. Those who had not been wounded were called up again during the Korean War and then turned that great tradition of service over to my generation. Vietnam saw several cousins serving. The Cold War saw me, my brother, and more cousins serving our great country. I met my husband in the military. My generation also saw smaller, shorter conflicts and peacekeeping duty.

I entered the army on active duty in July 1978, after spending four years as a Reserve Officer Training Corps (ROTC) cadet in college. I stayed on active duty for over seven years and reverted to reserve status after I married my husband, Bill, but before we had our two sons, Chris and Kevin. My husband spent twenty years on active duty before retiring.

Several years ago, after more than twenty-seven years (spent on both active duty and as a reservist), I received my final promotion — to civilian! Finally, more time to devote to quilting! I have been a quilter for most of my adult life and I decided it was time to give a little back to the men and women with whom I have had the pleasure to serve.

This book is the first in a series of *Making Quilts to Honor Those Who Serve*, with this one honoring the officer ranks. The series covers the commissioned officer ranks from O-1, Second Lieutenant to O-6, and Colonel; it does not include the general officer ranks. I have spread the quilt themes out among the five services: the Army, Navy, Air Force, Marines, and Coast Guard. Although most of my experiences deal with the Army, I hope I do justice to the army's four sister services. Those unfamiliar with military ranks and structure, please refer to Chapter 8: Military Ranks.

Chapter One

QUILTING TIPS

The six major quilts in this book are military themed, so there is a preponderance of patriotic (red, white, and blue), field (green and brown), air (blues), and sea (blue, yellow, and gray) colors. At the end of each chapter is a mini-gallery of quilts based on the pattern highlighted by that chapter. Some carry on with the patriotic and military theme with their colors, and several show the versatility of the patterns to create a wide range of quilts using various color themes.

The six quilts rely upon either two or three major colors.

When making your quilt from this book, choose the pattern first and then choose the fabrics. After constructing the blocks, it is a lot of fun to lay them on the floor or put them up on a design wall and rotate them around several ways to create your own unique quilt top!

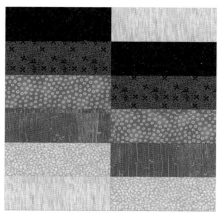

Most quilt books start with a chapter on basic quilt construction; if you need assistance in this area, refer to any quilt magazine or most quilting books. I have skipped this particular step.

1 Unless otherwise stated, **always** sew with a 1/4" seam.

2 If you are using similar colored or many fabrics, do the following: After sewing strips together, before cutting for the blocks, cut off the selvage edge and label or number the fabric so you have no question about which fabric goes where.

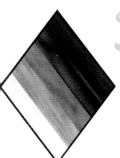

3 Several of the patterns in this book (Chapters 2, 6, 7) have fabric cut on the bias (diagonally across the grain of the fabric). I would strongly advise you to use spray starch or sizing to keep the blocks from stretching before being sewn together.

4 Appliqué Tips: The appliqués in this book instruct you to use the needle turn method. However, appliqué can be done either of two ways:

A. The first method is needle turn. Trace the pattern onto the right side of the fabric with a soft pencil/chalk pencil. Cut the pattern out, leaving a 1/4" allowance to turn under. Pin the appliqué to fabric. Following the pencil marks, turn the fabric under with the needle and stitch under.

B. The second method is to press a double-backed adhesive, such as Steam-A-Seam2®, to the wrong side of the appliqué fabric. Follow all the adhesive directions that come on the package. Note: When using double-backed adhesives, it is not necessary to add a 1/4" when cutting out the appliqué.

1 Squaring

Squaring a quilt is perhaps **the most important step in quilt construction**. Proper s*quaring* will ensure the quilt can hang and lay flat. *Squaring* should occur during all the final phases of quilt top construction. Why *square* a quilt? Because no pattern survives exactly as it is drawn/written — just as no military contingency plan survives first contact with outside (enemy) forces. The quilt can suffer from improper measuring and cutting of fabrics and not sewing seams at exactly 1/4" all through the quilt top. Also, working on the bias of the fabric can alter the shape of the quilt, as can the actual quilting itself. In order to remedy this potential disaster, *please, please* read the following and square your quilt! Always measure and re-measure before cutting. As my husband would tell our boys when we were building our barn, measure twice, cut once. Below are potential disaster points if ignored!

A. Quilt tops should be measured and *squared* before any borders are cut. This will ensure borders go on easily. This is especially true if any of your blocks have raw edges that were cut on the bias.

B. Measuring and *squaring* is not usually necessary after the borders are sewn on — unless the borders have raw edge bias cuts.

C. After the top has been constructed, sandwiched, and quilted, *square* your quilt again before sewing on the binding. Quilting, especially machine-quilting, can cause stretching and distortion of the quilt.

2 Squaring a Quilt

A. The "square quilt" is a quilt where all four sides are the same length (a=a) (**figure 1**).

About 15-20% of all quilts are square in shape; many of the block quilts in this book can be made as square quilts. An easy method to *square* a "square quilt" is to measure all four sides. They should all be the same length.

Now, fold the quilt in half, corner to corner, both ways (**figure 2**). The smaller the quilt, the more important it is for all the sides to be the same length and for the corner-to-corner measurements to be the same length. If one or more sides are too long or the corner-to-corner measurement is off, merely trim off the excess in *small increments*. Trim in small increments and re-measure constantly. The larger a quilt is (large lap to bed-size), it is acceptable to be off by as much as 1/4" on any one side. Any measurement larger than a 1/4" and the quilt should be trimmed in *small increments*.

The last measurement — the actual *squaring* — is to measure from corner to corner both ways (**figure 3**). These measurements must be equal or, in the case of a large quilt, within 1/4" of each other or the quilt is not "squared."

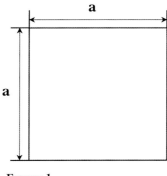

FIGURE 1

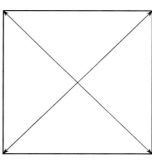

FIGURE 2

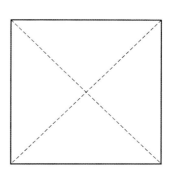

FIGURE 3

B. The "rectangle quilt" is a quilt where the two opposite sides are the same length, but a≠b. About 75-80% of all quilts are rectangular, as are all of the original six quilts in this book. To *square* a rectangle quilt, measure all four sides. The two pair of opposite sides should be the same measurement (a=a, b=b) (**figure 4**).

Even though the top and bottom measure the same and the left and right sides measure the same, the quilt is not yet *squared*. You must measure the quilt from corner-to-corner both ways (**figure 5**). If these two measurements are not the same, the quilt is not *square*. Squaring the quilt is the same as above: trim off the excess in *small increments* and measure constantly. Small quilts should have equal corner-to-corner measurements; larger quilts can vary by about 1/4". If the quilt measures the same for both corner-to-corner measurements, then the quilt is *square*!

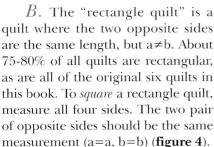

FIGURE 4

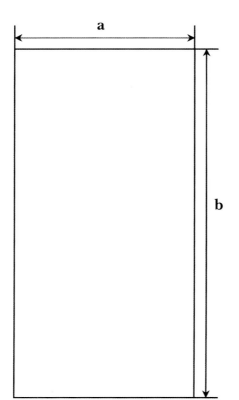

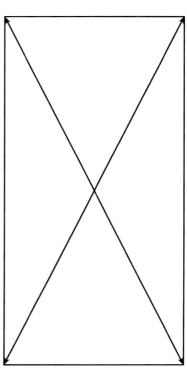

FIGURE 5

3 Borders

Before cutting border fabric for any quilt, first *square* your quilt. Before cutting borders, a number of potential disaster points are lurking in your sewing room and with your quilt. Working on the bias can throw off a block or

quilt's size and shape, improper measuring and cutting of fabrics can throw off a block or quilt's size, some poorly manufactured fabrics (read: cheap fabrics) that stretch and fray can throw off a block or quilt's size or shape, and my most famous culprit (something I'm never guilty of — oh, no), not sewing an exact 1/4" seam can throw off a block or quilt's size and shape.

While reading the recommended border size cuts, always measure *both* opposing sides (whether working on a square or rectangular quilt) and cut them the same length even

though they might be off by fractions of an inch. Pin the borders onto the quilt top and do some selective "easing" of fabric through the machine foot.

A. While measuring for the borders, start with the long sides first. However, sometimes it is more advantageous to start with the shorter side, so always follow the pattern instructions. Measure the sides, cut the fabric, and sew the border on the two sides.

B. Measure the shorter sides (with longer sides already sewn on), cut fabric, and sew.

C. Repeat this method for all subsequent borders.

D. After constructing the borders, sandwich the quilt and quilt. *Square* the quilt.

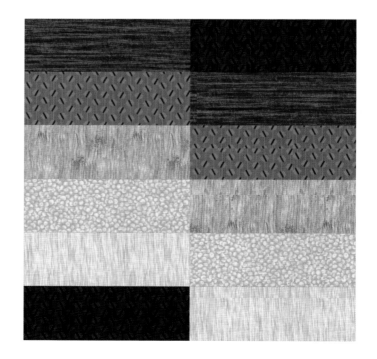

4 Binding

Finally! We are ready for the binding! Modern consensus no longer dictates binding must be cut on the bias (who made that a rule anyway?).

A. To make binding, cut your strips either 2-1/4" or 2-1/2" wide. The 1/4" either way is a personal preference; I prefer the smaller cut, as I like my binding tight, but many people like the larger cut. Join the strips, right side together, at a 90° angle, fold the corner, and press (**figure 6**). Stitch on the pressed line. Press the seam open (this decreases the layers of fabric) and trim to 1/4".

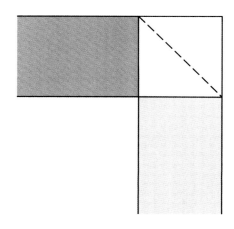

FIGURE 6

B. Lay out flat again and press (**figure 7**).

C. Fold the binding in half, right sides out, and, using 1/4" seam, sew the binding to the front of the quilt. Fold the binding over the raw edge of the quilt and hand or machine stitch it to the back of the quilt.

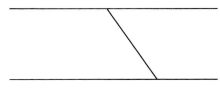

FIGURE 7

5 Labels

Every quilt has a story or purpose, so document it! A quilt without a label is an unfinished quilt.

There are entire books about making labels for quilts, so I won't go into the many methods here — just the method I use.

A. I document the pertinent information: *Title*, *Constructed by*, *Quilted by* (if done by someone else), *Purpose*, *Date*, and *Place*. See example below:

Colonel's Star
Designed and constructed by Renelda
Peldunas-Harter
Quilted by Carolyn Goins cpgDesigns.com
For the book *From Ensign's Bars to Colonel's
Stars*
July 2010
Purcellville, VA

B. For both handwritten and computer-generated labels, I use either unbleached muslin or dyed muslin. To create a handwritten label, use a non-running, indelible ink. If

making a computer-generated label, use a laser printer. Set the ink by using a hot iron and pressing the lettering.

C. Attach the label in the lower left or right corner of the quilt.

Chapter Two

ENSIGN'S BARS (O-1)

There are basically three ways to become a commissioned officer in the active military. Graduation from a military academy, such as West Point (as my husband did), Annapolis (for Navy and Marines), the Air Force Academy or the Coast Guard Academy, is one way to receive a commission. A second way is to graduate from a Reserve Officer Training Corps (ROTC), which are at select colleges and universities (as I did). A third way to receive a commission is for an enlisted member to apply for and be accepted to Officer Candidate School (OCS), as my brother, Ken, did. Graduate from any one of the three and you become an O-1 (a "Butter bar"), a 2-L-T (a Second Lieutenant), or an Ensign. The rank of O-1 is designated by a single gold bar.

As a young second lieutenant, I was commissioned a Women's Army Corps (WAC) officer and detailed to the Chemical Corps branch. The year I was commissioned, the WACs were on their way out and women were fully integrating into the combat support and service support branches of the army. President Truman racially integrated the military after WWII, doing away with all separate black or white units. In the late 1970s, the same thing happened for women. I was the only one of my college buddies who received equal pay for equal work — that was a big deal in 1978!

Although trained as a Chemical officer, I found myself with a Graves Registration (GR) platoon in a Field Service Company. The GR platoon recovers human remains lost in the line of duty (generally on a battlefield), identifies and processes the remains, and turns the remains over to mortuary collection points. Yes, I know, there is another book about just that assignment (so many assignments, so little time to write about)!

Since Fort Lee, Virginia, is close to the state medical examiner's office in Richmond, we traveled there most days and assisted the medical examiners with autopsies. Eventually, Fort Lee received its own pathologist and our commute was shortened considerably.

I really enjoyed my time spent as an LT, being a platoon leader and learning the ropes from my commander and First Sergeant. I was soon re-assigned up to battalion to be the G-2 (intelligence officer), with my major extra duty being the battalion unit status officer (USR). The only reason I was "promoted" to battalion was because, since I was a chemical officer, it was assumed I could add and the monthly USR involved plenty of calculations. In every battalion or brigade, the chemical officer was usually the USR officer.

One of the best things about being a commissioned officer is that you have the privilege of administering the oath of service to newly enlisted, re-enlisting, and newly commissioned officers and officiating at the promotions of other service members. Being eight months pregnant and not in an active status, my husband gladly assumed the honor of pinning Ensign Bars on my brother, Ken, when he was commissioned an O-1 (an Ensign) out of Officer Candidate School in 1986.

In honor of my brother, and all the other men and women who earned their commission by going through OCS to become an Ensign or 2nd Lieutenant, *Ensign's Bars* is dedicated to you! To honor the grade of O-1 in the Navy and Coast Guard, I used white to represent the summer uniform, shades of gray from submarines, sub-tenders, aircraft carriers — all the seaworthy vessels — and the dark blue of the naval and Coast Guard winter uniform. The shape reminds me of a mariner's knot.

14

Ensign's Bars, 50" x 80". Designed and pieced by Renelda Peldunas-Harter. Quilted by Carolyn Perry Goins.

Ensign's Bars

Level: Intermediate

Finished Quilt: 50" x 80"

Finished Block: Skewed 11-1/4" x 19-1/2"

MATERIALS

(Yardage based on 42"-wide fabric)

- 3/4 yd. deep dark blue for block
- 1-3/4 yd. dark blue for block and outer border
- 1-1/2 yd. dark gray for block and inner border
- 3/4 yd. gray for block
- 3/4 yd. white for block
- 60° ruler—most 12-1/2" x 12-1/2" or 6-1/2" x 6-1/2" squares have 60° markings

CUTTING & SEWING

(All measurements include 1/4" seam)

1 Cut 10 each 2-1/2" x 42" strips from each color and sew strips together to form 10 strip sets (**figure 1**). Keep the white strip on top when cutting.

2 Press toward the dark color and press straight; bowing will throw off block size.

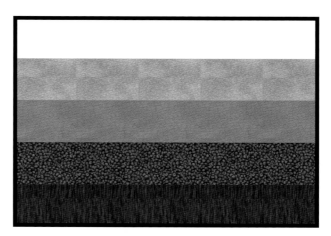

FIGURE 1

FIGURE 2: LEFT (L) CUT BLOCK

FIGURE 3: RIGHT (R) CUT BLOCK

FIGURE 4

1 For blocks, use 6 strip sets (set other 4 strip sets aside). Half of the strip sets (3) will be cut to the left (L) (**figure 2**) and half of the strip sets (3) will be cut to the right (R) (**figure 3**). Each strip set will yield 3 blocks (total: 9 right, 9 left).

2 Using the 60° ruler, cut each unit (60°) from corner top to bottom of unit. Refer to diagram (**figure 4**) and measure 12" over from the cut on both the top and bottom, cut. Do this three times, as each unit yields three blocks. Cut half of the strip sets to the right (R) and half of the strip sets to the left (L), yielding a total of 9 right blocks and 9 left blocks. Remember to always keep the white fabric on top.

QUILT CONSTRUCTION

FIGURE 5

1 Refer to the diagram (**figure 5**) as you lay the blocks out or place on a design wall.

2 Lay out all 18 blocks, being careful of the pattern.

3 Of the 4 remaining strips, which were set aside, use as follows:

A. Half diamond blocks at the top and bottom: Determine which type block (right or left) will finish the top or bottom patterns and cut 3 blocks (one block cut horizontally will work on both the top and bottom). Cut the full blocks in half horizontally (**figure 6**) and place on top and bottom of quilt top.

B. Half diamond blocks for sides: Again, determine which type block (right or left) will finish the sides of the quilt top. Cut 3 full size blocks for both sides, and then cut each block vertically (**figure 7**) to create a straight edge.

C. Corner blocks: All sides will be straight except for two corner blocks. Cut an additional top/bottom block, cut in half horizontally, orient to corner, and cut vertically to create 90° corners (**figure 8**).

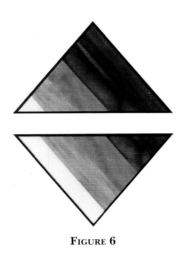

FIGURE 6

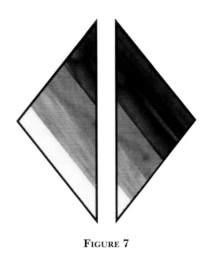

FIGURE 7

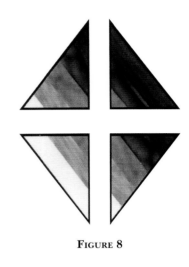

FIGURE 8

ASSEMBLE THE QUILT TOP

1 Make sure all the blocks have been cut and placed before sewing together.

2 Sew the diagonal blocks together into rows, starting with the longer rows first (**figure 9**).

3 To sew the rows together, start in the middle with a longer row and work out to the right to the shorter rows, completing half of the quilt top.

4 Again, start in the middle and sew the shorter rows together, working to the left and completing the other half of the quilt top.

5 Sew the two halves together.

FIGURE 9

1 Before cutting and working on the borders, first check out Chapter 1, Finishing Phase, Squaring a quilt #2 and Borders #3.

2 Square your quilt and then measure and cut your borders, 2 opposite sides at a time.

3 Because of all the bias edges, the measurements can be off as much as 1/2". Accurate cutting of the inner border and plenty of pinning the border onto the quilt will ensure proper sizing.

4 Inner Border: Cut 2 strips 70" x 2-1/4" and cut 2 strips 43-1/2" x 2-1/4".

5 Outer Border: Cut 2 strips 73-1/2" x 3-1/2" and cut 2 strips 49-1/2" x 3-1/2".

6 For binding construction, check out Chapter 1, Finishing Phase, Binding #4.

7 Cut binding 2-1/2" x 312".

Ensign's Bars Gallery

Carolyn Perry Goins challenged herself to take the "Ensign's" block and create a totally different effect by running the blocks in a horizontal flow instead of a vertical flow. The result is *Raspberry Fizz*, a pink and teal delight! Carolyn's quilt measures 62" x 80" and was machine-pieced and quilted using batiks. Carolyn's connection to the military is her husband, who retired after 27 years as a Signal Officer. Their journey together started with the California National Guard and continued through tours of duty in West Germany and Turkey, as well as several state-side assignments.

Carolyn is a pattern designer and quilting teacher. She is also my "go to" person when I have a question about hand- or machine-piecing, machine-quilting, or any other general knowledge quilting questions. You can keep up with Carolyn on her blog at www.cpgDesigns.blogspot.com.

Raspberry Fizz, 62" x 80". Machine-pieced and quilted by Carolyn Perry Goins.

Red, White & Blue, 55" x 75". Machine-pieced by Catherine Snyder and quilted by Pat Fitzpatrick.

Catherine Snyder has recently returned with her husband from the Middle East and is a very active participant with the Quilts of Valor Foundation. This quilt is named *Red, White & Blue* and measures 55" x 75". She made both this quilt and the one following specifically for the Quilts of Valor program. Catherine has been a volunteer for the program for several years as a quilter, a long-armer, and even for a short term as its Director. Quilted by Pat Fitzpatrick of Finely Finished Quilting.

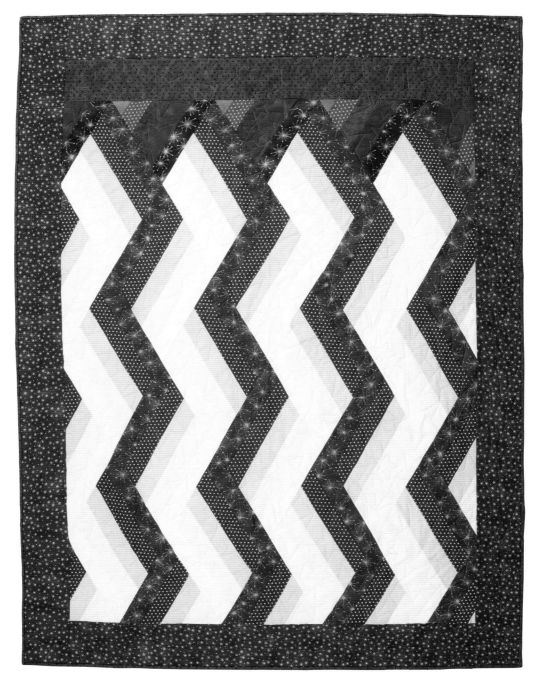

Our Flag, 55" x 65". Machine-pieced by Catherine Snyder and quilted by Pat Fitzpatrick.

The second of Catherine Snyder's quilts for this book is *Our Flag*. It is 55" x 75" and it will be given to the Quilts of Valor program. All quilts made for the Quilts of Valor program must be at least 55" x 65". The quilts are designed to cover a member, providing comfort and helping with the healing process, instead of hanging on a wall. They are made with love and respect in the hope that the service members will realize their sacrifices and experiences will not be forgotten. Quilts of Valor are meant to be historical quilts, to be handed down through families as heirlooms. Find out more about the Quilts of Valor Foundation by visiting www. QOVF.org. Quilted by Pat Fitzpatrick of Finely Finished Quilting.

Chapter Three

LIEUTENANT'S PLATOON (O-2)

In the Army, Air Force, and Marines, the grade O-2 is a 1st Lieutenant. In the Navy and Coast Guard, the rank of O-2 is a Lieutenant, junior grade (LTJG). A 1LT, as it is abbreviated in the Army, is usually a platoon leader. Platoons are at the bottom of the basic pyramid structure of the Army and Marines. Platoons will have anywhere from twenty-five to sixty soldiers, non-commissioned officers (NCOs), one platoon sergeant, and one platoon leader. The platoon is where officers are trained to lead, manage, and learn their job — be it to fight, to support the fighters directly, or to provide service support to the fighters. The rank of O-2 is designated by a single silver bar.

I finally managed to return to the 16th Field Service Company from battalion to take over the Chemical Decontamination Platoon (Decon). There were only four active duty Decon platoons and no Chemical Companies at the time, so we were still with the Quartermaster units. Decon platoons had a lot of equipment, carried around on 2-1/2 or 5-ton trucks, and, when we set up our field operation, it covered many acres. We spent a lot of time out in the field, away from ringing telephones, "Hey–you" duties, and the battalion staff.

My 1LT days also bring back memories of the last vestiges of the Women Army Corp (WAC) fatigues — contoured to fit the supposedly less-active female soldier. The role of women in the military was evolving, as females were admitted to the military academies and it was discovered that the myth of women possessing no upper body strength was just that, a myth. The physical fitness test (PT) became more standardized (cut from five events that were different for males and females to the same three events: push-ups, sit-ups, and a two-mile run) and the fatigues transformed into the unisex woodland BDU (Battle Dress Uniform). In my mind, the rank of 1LT will always be seen in shades of khaki, brown, and green, and organized into compartmented sections — hence the quilt in this chapter.

In search of more adventure, I volunteered for a one-year assignment to the Republic of Korea (ROK). I was assigned to the Division Support Command (DISCOM) as the Chemical officer. Our division-wide chemical meetings came around the fifteenth of each month as all the brigade Chemical officers were also the Unit Status Report (USR) officers — math! (Check out the previous chapter for more information about USR.) We spent a lot of time out in the field and traveling to far-flung units all around the ROK (pronounced "rock"). During the winter, the wind blew from the north over the mountains directly into our area. Division policy was for no running when the temperature outside was below 17°F. The year I was there, we didn't run for over four months! It took over five minutes to put on enough layers of clothing to be able to go outside. Monsoons came in the late summer and typhoons in the fall, bringing with them constant wetness and raging storms.

The children's orphanage was the usual benefactor of the many betting pools that went on during the typhoon season. For example, what date/time do you think the large one-hundred-year-old tree will finally blow into the roof of the Officer's Club? The Chaplain always held the money and the date/time sheet and was the final arbiter of who actually won (these could be tense competitions!). No one actually ever claimed the money; betting competitions were just an excuse to raise money for the children's orphanage.

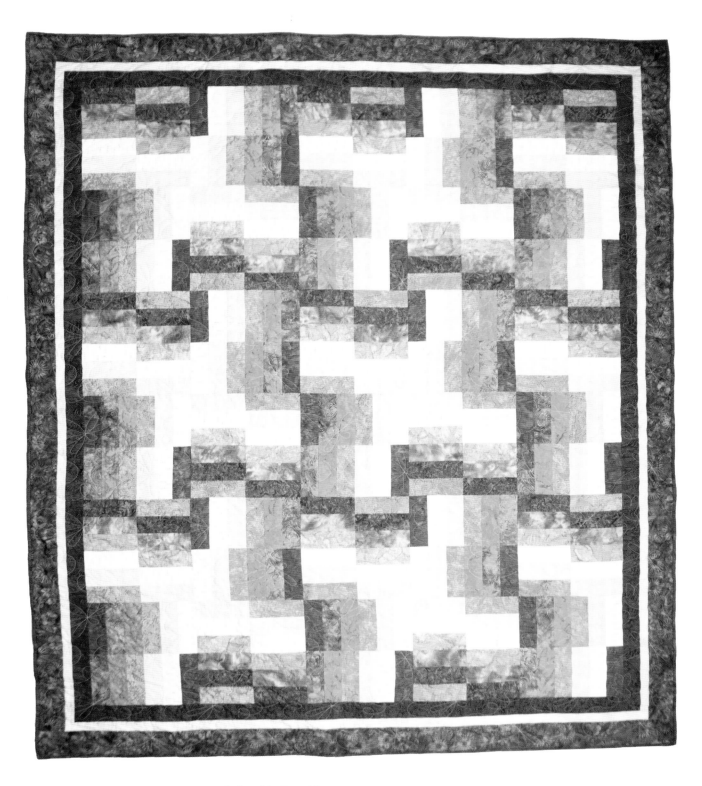

LT's Platoon, 72" x 84". Designed and pieced by Renelda Peldunas-Harter. Quilted by Carolyn Perry Goins.

Lieutenant's Platoon

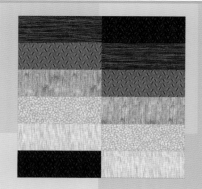

LEVEL: Beginner

FINISHED QUILT: 72" x 84"

FINISHED BLOCK: 12" x 12"

MATERIALS

(Yardages based on 42"-wide fabric)

- 1-1/2 yd. each of dark brown for Brown Block and inner border
- 1/2 yd. of 2 medium browns for Brown Block
- 1 yd. each of 2 medium light browns for Brown Block and Green Block

- 1-1/2 yd. of light brown for Brown Block, Green Block, and middle border
- 1-1/2 yd. each of dark green for Green Block and outer border
- 1/2 yd. each of 2 medium greens for Green Block

CUTTING & SEWING

(All measurements include a 1/4" seam)

(a) dark brown
(b) medium dark brown
(c) medium brown
(d) medium brown
(e) medium light brown
(f) light brown
(g) dark green
(h) medium dark green
(i) medium green

Brown Block
for constructing
columns 1 & 2

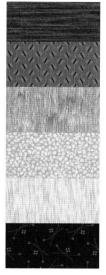

FIGURE 1
Column 1

FIGURE 2
Column 2

1 Using fabrics (a) through (f), cut six 2-1/2" x 42" strips.

2 Divide the strips into two piles, with an equal number of strips and colors in each.

3 Sew the fabric strips together in the following order (b, c, d, e, f, a), making 3 entire strip sets (**figure 1**) for column 1. Strip sets measure 12-1/2" x 42".

4 Sew the remaining fabric strips together in the following order (a, b, c, d, e, f), making 3 sets (**figure 2**) for column 2. Press both towards the darkest brown color; this will help when sewing the columns together. There are now 3 sets of 12-1/2" x 42" for each column.

Green Block
for constructing
columns 1 & 2

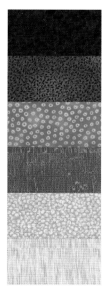
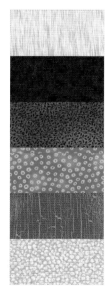

FIGURE 3
Column 1

FIGURE 4
Column 2

1 Using fabrics (d) through (i), cut six 2-1/2" x 42" strips.

2 Divide strips into two piles, with an equal number of strips and colors in each.

3 Sew the fabric strips together in the following order (g, h, i, d, e, f) for column 1 (**figure 3**).

4 Sew remaining fabric strips together in the following order (f, g, h, i, d, e) for column 2 (**figure 4**). Press toward the medium brown (d) for both columns. There are now 3 sets of 12-1/2" x 42" for each column.

BLOCK CONSTRUCTION

1 Keep the Brown Block cuts and columns separated from the Green Block cuts and columns.

2 Cut each column set into 12-1/2" x 6-1/2" unit strips for a total of fifteen 12-1/2" x 6-1/2" columns (getting 5 columns per strip).

3 Brown Block: Match up the unit strips for the Brown Block by placing one Column 1 and Column 2 together (**figure 5**). Line up together and sew to form the Brown Block.

4 Green Block: Match up the unit strips for the Green Block by placing one Column 1 and Column 2 together (**figure 6**). Line up and sew to form Green Block.

5 There are now 15 green and 15 brown 12-1/2" x 12-1/2" blocks.

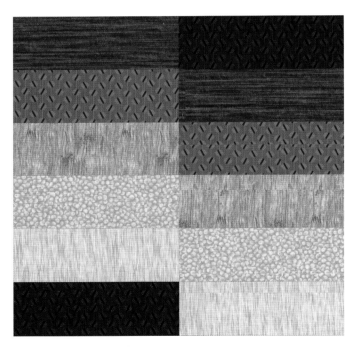

FIGURE 5: Brown Block

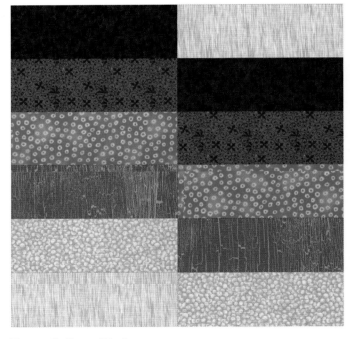

FIGURE 6: Green Block

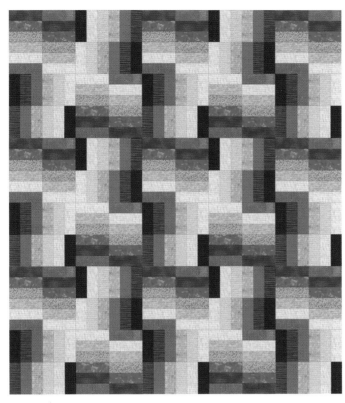

FIGURE 7

1 Refer to the quilt assembly diagram to layout the blocks (**figure 7**) in 6 rows with 5 blocks per row.

2 Alternate Green Blocks with Brown Blocks. Refer to diagram for orientation placement: Green Blocks are all facing up; Brown Blocks are all rotated to the left or right 90°.

3 Sew the rows across, starting at the top, constructing 6 rows.

4 Sew rows together.

BORDERS & BINDING

1 Before cutting and working on the borders, first check out Chapter 1, Finishing Phase, Squaring a quilt #2 and Borders #3.

2 Square your quilt and then measure and cut your borders, 2 opposite sides at a time.

3 Inner Border: Cut 2 each 2-1/2" x 73" and 2 each 2-1/2" x 65".

4 Middle Border: Cut 2 each 1-1/2" x 77" and 2 each 1-1/2" x 67".

5 Outer Border: Cut 2 each 3-1/2" x 79" and 2 each 3-1/2" x 72".

6 Cut binding 2-1/4" x 320".

LT's Platoon Gallery

Pinked is a great example of how different colors can change the look of a quilt. Dolores Gattuso Goodson used pinks, grays, blacks, and whites to give this quilt a contemporary look. The quilt measures 45" x 45", is machine-pieced, and both hand- and machine-quilted by Dolores. Dolores has ties with the military. Her father, TSgt Anthony Gattuso, Sr., is a 24-year Air Force veteran who started off as a baker and retired as a Military Police Officer. Dolores was born at Ladd AFB in Fairbanks, Alaska, and her three siblings were born at Lackland AFB in San Antonio, Texas, Wiesbaden AFB in Wiesbaden, Germany, and Langley AFB in Hampton, Virginia. You can keep up with Dolores' blog at www.deeroodesigns.blogspot.com.

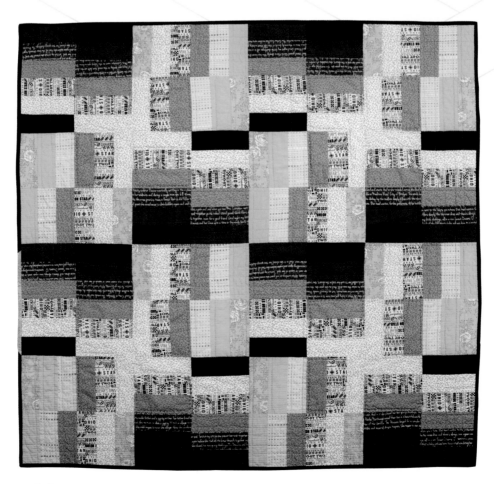

Pinked, 45" x 45". Machine-pieced and hand- and machine-quilted by Dolores Gattuso Goodson.

Calm Seas, 55" x 55". Machine-pieced and quilted by Renelda Peldunas-Harter.

Calm Seas uses various batiks in the turquoise and blue pallete. Pieced and quilted by Renelda Peldunas-Harter, this 55" x 55" quilt demonstrates how combining different colors and adding a splash of black and gray can give the basic quilt an entirely different appearance.

Chapter Four

CAPTAIN'S COMPANY (O-3)

Captains in the Army and Marines are the real officer workhorses. If you want to work eighteen-hour days, not see your families, get ulcers, give ulcers, and start the gray hair thing, then the rank of O-3 is for you! Captains (CPT) are given Companies to command. Lieutenants run platoons, but captains *command*. Companies are anywhere from three to five platoons, depending on the company type. The rank of O-3 in the Army, Marines, and Air Force is captain; in the Navy and Coast Guard, the rank is lieutenant (LT).

Back in the old days (Horse Cavalry to WWII), the company commander was referred to as the "Old Man" because a large majority of officers rose to the rank of captain and stayed there until they died or retired. Hence, companies were literally run by old men. To my great relief, I was never in line to command a company. As the senior LT in the company (the commander was gone for a week on business), I was left in temporary command of the 16th Field Service Company. As I entered the Orderly Room to speak with the 1st Sergeant, I overheard two troops talking in the hall about me, one saying, "I guess that LT Peldunas is the old man for the next week." I had finally arrived. At the ripe old age of 23,

I was the old man! (Surely, the forerunner to actually being "Da'man.")

The ranks of O-1 to O-3 are considered "company grade" or "junior grade" because most of the tactical work is accomplished at the company level. Companies usually do not operate independently.

It seemed like half of my military career was spent as a Captain. I spent a few years as a chemical and biological planner at the Rapid Deployment Joint Task Force (RDJTF) in Tampa, Florida. The RDJTF was formed as a result of several events: the hostage crisis in Iran in 1979 and the Soviet invasion of Afghanistan in the same year. The United States had no headquarters to deal with any kind of crisis in the Middle East and so the RDJTF was born. While I was assigned in Tampa, the RDJTF was upgraded to an actual command and renamed the United States Central Command (CENTCOM). Those were exciting times! I deployed to Egypt for an exercise with SFC Jimmy Jenkins because the boss didn't think the two of us could get into trouble in the middle of the desert. He might have been right or wrong — the after action reports are still classified. In preparation for the deployment, I studied Arabic and could give directions and make our needs known, but all that study was in vain: our Arabic-speaking drivers wouldn't talk to a woman in Arabic if a non-Arabic speaking man was present! Poor SFC Jenkins had to communicate using his hands and gestures. We did get to see a lot of Soviet equipment by going into the desert and visiting line units.

Bill and I got married in Tampa and then we moved to West Point, New York, for a joint assignment. I was assigned to Readiness Group Stewart as the Chemical Officer. SFC Don Honeywell and I were the Nuclear Biological Chemical (NBC) team and we spent many long days with reserve and Army National Guard units making sure they were ready to deploy. Our territory covered everything from Albany, New York, down to and including New York City and all of Long Island. It was very interesting working with the "weekend warriors." Little did I realize I would spend the next twenty years as one!

At this rank, I got off active duty and became a reserve officer. I became the operations officer of a mobile army reserve hospital and finally got to work with a lot of female officers (nurses) and troops.

I designed this quilt to honor the Air Force (blues) and the Marines (reds). The deceptively simple design appears to have many layers, just like the rank of captain. The rank of O-3 wears two silver bars.

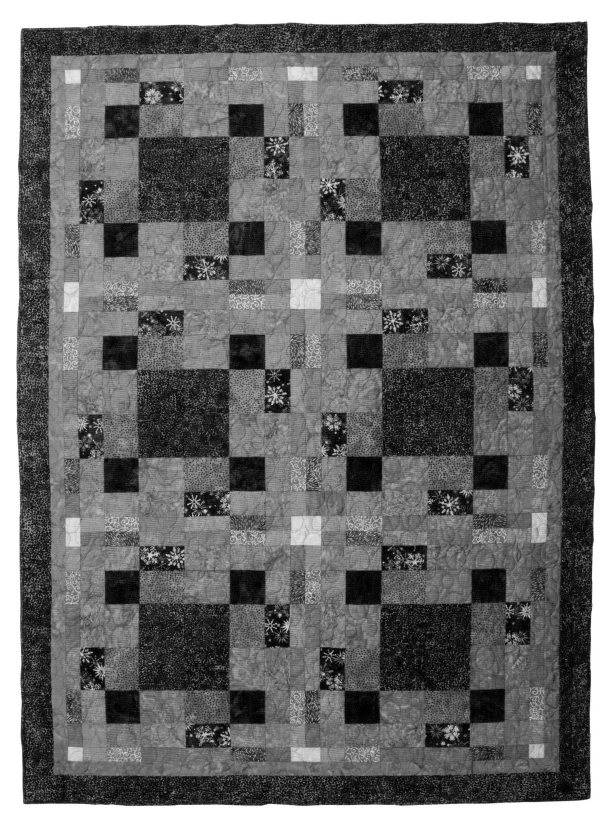

Captain's Company, 57" x 81". Designed and pieced by
Renelda Peldunas-Harter. Quilted by Carolyn Perry Goins.

Captain's Company

LEVEL: Beginner
FINISHED QUILT: 57" x 81"
FINISHED BLOCK: 12" x 12"

MATERIALS

(Yardages based on 43"-wide fabric)

- 1/8 yd. of light blue (A) for blocks
- 1/4 yd. red (B), medium blue (C), red (E), medium blue (I), red (M) for blocks
- 1/2 yd. red (D), red (G), medium blue (H), red (J), dark blue (N), red (O) for blocks
- 3/4 yd. red (L), dark blue (P) for blocks
- 1 yd. medium blue (F) blocks and inner border
- 1-1/2 yd. dark blue (K) for blocks and outer border

CUTTING & SEWING

(All measurements include a 1/4" seam)

Cut and sew each column separately:

1 Column I:
Cut 2 strips from each fabric:

(A) Light blue: Cut 2" x 43"
(B) Red: Cut 3" x 43"
(C) Medium blue: Cut 4" x 43"
(D) Red: Cut 5" x 43"

Sew into 2 strip sets (**FIGURE 1**) and cut twenty-four 2" strips (**FIGURE 2**) from each. Press toward red fabric.

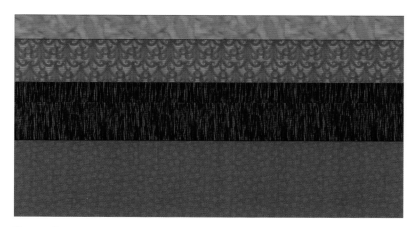

FIGURE 1

FIGURE 2

2 *Column II:*
Cut 3 strips from each fabric:

(E) Red: Cut 2" x 43"
(F) Medium blue: Cut 3" x 43"
(G) Red: Cut 4" x 43"
(H) Dark blue: Cut 5" x 43"

Sew into 3 sets (**FIGURE 3**) and cut twenty-four 3" strips (**FIGURE 4**) from each. Press toward red fabric.

FIGURE 3

FIGURE 4

3 *Column III:*
Cut 4 strips from each fabric:

(I) Medium blue: Cut 2" x 43"
(J) Red: Cut 3" x 43"
(K) Dark blue: Cut 4" x 43"
(L) Red: Cut 5" x 43"

Sew into 4 units and cut twenty-four 4" strips (**FIGURE 5**) from each. Press toward red fabric.

FIGURE 5

4 *Column IV:*
Cut 4 strips from each fabric:

(M) Red: Cut 2" x 43"
(N) Dark blue: Cut 3" x 43"
(O) Red: Cut 4" x 43"
(P) Dark blue: Cut 5" x 43"

Sew into 5 units and cut twenty-four 5" strips (**FIGURE 6**) from each. Press toward red fabric.

FIGURE 6

BLOCK CONSTRUCTION

1 By pressing red seams up/ blue down, joining columns will be simple as the junctions will ease together.

2 Arrange combined column strips and sew as follows:
2a. Column I to Column II

2b. Column III to Column IV
2c. Sew column I & II to Column III & IV (**FIGURE 7**)

3 Construct a total of 24 blocks.

FIGURE 7

ASSEMBLE THE QUILT TOP

Refer to quilt picture for block placement (**FIGURE 8**).

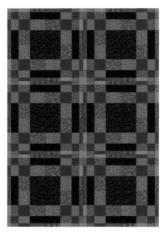

FIGURE 8

BORDERS

1 Before cutting and working on the borders, first check out Chapter 1, Finishing Phase: Squaring a quilt #2 and Borders #3.

2 Square your quilt and then measure and cut your borders, 2 opposite sides at a time.

3 Inner Border: Cut 2 each 2" x 72-1/2" and 2" x 52".

4 Outer Border: Cut 2 each 3-1/2" x 77" and 3-1/2" x 58".

5 For binding construction, refer to Chapter 1 Finishing Phase: Binding #4.

6 Cut binding 2-1/2" x 350".

Captain's Company Gallery

For Carol Cushman Casey, making *In the Army* brought back childhood memories of when her dad was an NCO in the Corps of Engineers stationed in Greenland. Casey chose olive green as the main fabric because it reminded her of "Army"! The floral fabrics in the quilt honor the women who serve beside the men. The center of each block group is a large red cross, which has a dual meaning: to honor the American Red Cross and to honor the medics. The small red/white blocks represent ships that would transport soldiers and supplies. The red and white pinwheels symbolize the helicopters (whirlybirds) that Casey watched take off and land as a child.

It is amazing to me how one person can take an essentially simple 16 patch block, add a little imagination, and come up with such a stunning quilt! This 65" x 93" quilt was pieced by Carol Cushman Casey and quilted by Kathy Shifman.

In the Army, 65" x 93".
Machine-pieced by Carol Cushman Casey, and machine-quilted by Kathy Shifman.

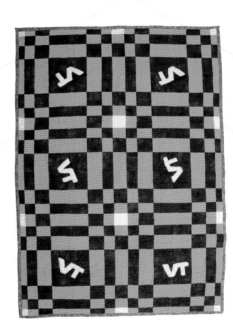

Old College Try, 48" x 71".
Machine-pieced, hand- and machine-quilted by Linda Burke.

Virginia Tech alumni and their families will recognize the distinctive colors of Linda Burke's *Old College Try*. This 48" x 71" quilt is the perfect graduation gift for the young man or woman going away to college. Linda went to Tech, as did our youngest son, Kevin, who graduated with a degree in Chemical Engineering. Linda machine-pieced and hand- and machined-quilted this unique Virginia Tech quilt. Go Hokies!

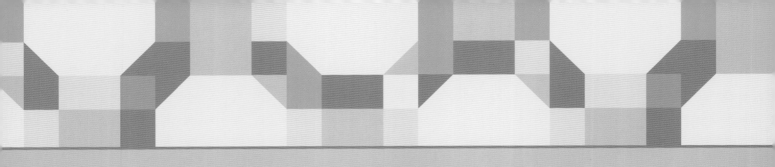

Chapter Five

MAJOR'S GOLD (O-4)

When you hit the rank of O-4, which is a Major (MAJ) in the Army, Air Force, and Marines and Lieutenant Commander (LCDR) in the Navy and Coast Guard, you become a "field grade" or "senior grade" officer. The ranks of O-4 through O-6 are officers who typically command units that can be expected to operate independently for short periods of time (i.e., infantry battalions, cavalry or artillery regiments, warships, air squadrons). Field officers also commonly fill staff positions of superior commands.

My experience as a major proved to be varied and even more interesting than previous experiences! I joined a reserve school and taught Command and General Staff College (CGSC) classes (mostly tactics and nuclear, biological, and chemical [NBC] operations — my specialties up until that time). I also started to realize that as a Chemical Officer, I could no longer find a job as a major. The reserves and National Guard had restructured placing all combat branches and direct combat support branches (chemical, engineers, military police, etc.) into the National Guard and placing the combat service support (medical, transportation, quartermaster, finance, etc.) into the reserves. With my husband still on active duty, there was no way I could continue to move around the country and find a spot in the Guard as a major or lieutenant colonel — those positions were reserved for officers who were "brought up" in that particular state's Guard system, not for some outsider.

Our family had just moved to the Northern Virginia area and I found a unit that I thought might prove to be both interesting and have the potential for advancement: Civil Affairs. At that time, it was very difficult to break into the Civil Affairs community — surprise, surprise! — but I managed to get in. In the mid-1990s, Civil Affairs and Psychological Operations were part of the Special Operations Command (SOC). We were required to do a timed six-mile forced march with fifty-five-pound ruck sacks, water survival and swimming tests, and land navigation at least once a year.

My two weeks at Fort Bragg for my Civil Affairs Advanced Course training happened to coincide with a large joint US-UK operation. All the Americans stayed off the roads because the Brits were driving around Fort Bragg (sometimes even on the right side of the road!), buying up as many TV sets and blue jeans as they could find. The most excitement occurred when our entire class was sequestered in an out-of-the-way, classified training area conducting our final field exam. We had just finished a three-day exercise, we were tired, it was dark outside, and we had just retired to our fifty-year-old barracks for what I hoped would be at least a few hours sleep. Because there were only two women in the class, we had a huge barracks building all to ourselves. Just as I was falling asleep, the combined US-UK Special Forces concluded the largest joint aerial nighttime assault operations since WWII — directly over our barracks. Helicopters were hovering, special ops troops were rappelling out of the helos all around our cantonment area, munitions were going off, smoke was everywhere, and that was just the first wave. Operations continued all night; no sleep was had. Welcome to Civil Affairs!

If you are a planner, strategist, coordinator, logistician, or large unit commander, then field grade ranks are the ranks for you! The rank of O-4 wears a gold oak leaf. The quilt in this chapter still has the greens and browns of the great outdoors with a few appliquéd oak leaves.

It's a MAJOR Quilt, 57" x 75".
Designed by Renelda Peldunas-Harter; machine-pieced
and hand-quilted by Leslie Heilman.

Major's Gold

LEVEL: Beginner

FINISHED QUILT: 57" x 75"

FINISHED BLOCK: 9" x 9"

MATERIALS

(Yardages based on 42"-wide fabric)

- 1-3/4 yd. medium gold/beige for large square (snowball square)
- 1 yd. light gold/beige for small square (9-patch square)

- 6-8 ea. assorted green and brown fat quarters or scrap fabric for small squares and rectangles
- 1 yd. dark green for border

CUTTING & SEWING

(All measurements include a 1/4" seam) This quilt is comprised of two blocks: a traditional snowball and a skewed 9-patch.

Snowball:

1 Cut 24 gold squares: 9-1/2" x 9-1/2"

2 Cut 96 green/brown squares: 2-3/4" x 2-3/4"

9-patch:

1 Cut 24 light gold squares: 5" x 5"

2 Cut 96 green/brown squares: 2-3/4" x 2-3/4"

3 Cut 96 green/brown rectangles: 5" x 2-3/4"

Snowball Block:

1 Select 4 random green/ brown small squares. Iron small squares in half vertically. Place small squares in each corner of 9" x 9" square (**FIGURE 1**). Stitch along iron line. Clip 1/4" away from the seam.

2 Iron flaps away from center, creating a square again (**FIGURE 2**). Repeat this 24 times, using 4 random green/ brown squares each time to create the 24 squares.

FIGURE 1

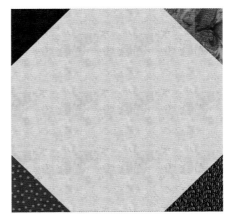

FIGURE 2

Nine-patch Block:

1 Each 9-patch block has:

(a) Center square 5" x 5"
(b) 4 green/brown rectangles 5" x 2-3/4"
(c) 4 green/brown squares 2-3/4" x 2-3/4"

2 Sew three separate strips (**FIGURE 3**):

(a) top strip (sq, rec, sq)
(b) middle strip (rec, lg sq, rec)
(c) bottom strip (sq, rec, sq)

FIGURE 3

3 Sew the three strips together (**FIGURE 4**).

4 Complete 24 Nine-patch squares.

5 Appliqué 5 gold leaves to random snowball blocks (**FIGURE 5**). The oak leaf appliqué appears at the end of this chapter (attachment 1). For assistance with appliquéing, refer to Chapter 1, Construction Phase.

FIGURE 4

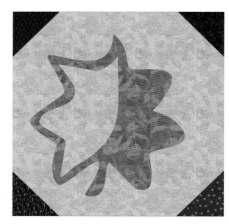

FIGURE 5

ASSEMBLY OF QUILT TOP

1 Refer to the quilt assembly diagram (**FIGURE 6**) to layout the blocks, alternating between snowball blocks and 9-patch.

2 Row 1 starts with a 9-patch block, alternate with a snowball block, sew the blocks together, 6 blocks in all. Sew 8 rows, ensuring the pattern of alternating blocks. Sew all the rows together.

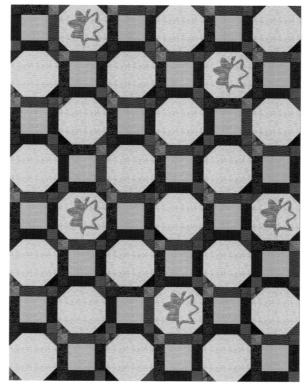

FIGURE 6

1 Before cutting and working on the borders, first check out Chapter 1, Finishing Phase, Squaring a quilt #2 and Borders #3.

2 Square your quilt and then measure and cut your borders, 2 opposite sides at a time.

3 Cut 2 strips for long side 2-1/2" x 71-1/4". Sew onto quilt.

4 Cut 2 strips for short side 2-1/2" x 57-1/2". Sew onto quilt.

5 For binding construction, refer to Chapter 1 Finishing Phase, Binding #4.

6 Cut binding 2-1/4" x 270". Sew binding onto quilt.

Major's Gold Gallery

Pat Peters did this miniature quilt called *Fall Gold*. Her focus fabric is an Australian fabric that has small 7-point leaves, suitable for the "major" theme; she chose the other fall colors to coordinate with the focus fabric.

Pat is a graduate of the Walter Reed Army Institute of Nursing (WRAIN) and served in the Army Nurse Corps in the late 1960s/early '70s, attaining the rank of Captain. Quilt pieced and quilted by Pat Holshue Peters.

Fall Gold, 28" x 37".
Hand-pieced and machine-quilted by Pat Holshue Peters.

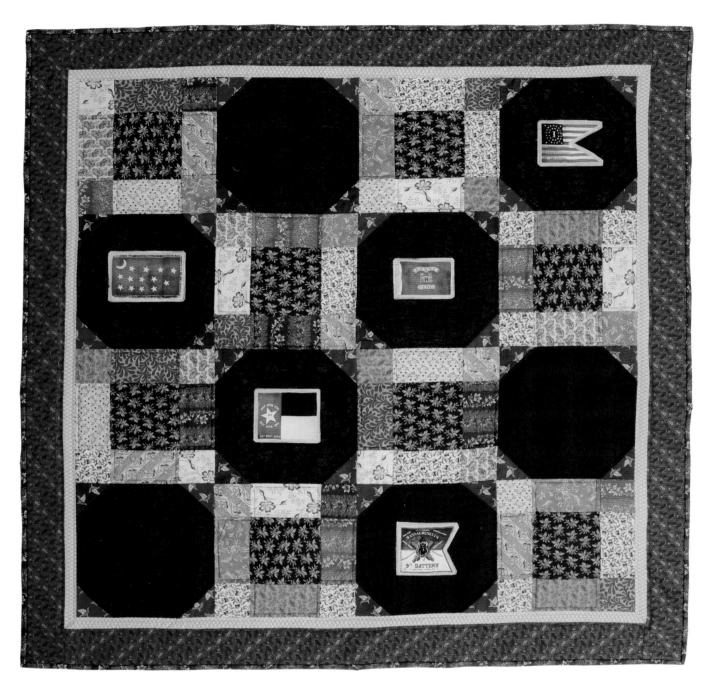

Civil War, 43" x 43".
Machine-pieced, appliquéd, and quilted by
Renelda Peldunas-Harter.

The beautiful fabric for this quilt
is courtesy of Windham Fabrics and
it is in The Gettysburg Civil War
VIII collection. The reds, blues, and
creams were the perfect showcase for
the many Civil War flags found in this
collection. The *Civil War* quilt is 43"
x 43" and was pieced and quilted by
Renelda Peldunas-Harter.

Oak leaf appliqué pattern.
Courtesy of Leslie Heilman.

Chapter Six

COMMANDER'S FLAGS (O-5)

The rank of O-5 is a Commander (CDR) in the Navy and Coast Guard and a Lieutenant Colonel (LTC) in the Army, Air Force, and Marines. This quilt is naval themed, using flag-shaped blocks that were used by the Navy and Coast Guard to communicate between navy ships, which are generally commanded by a Commander.

I really enjoyed the rank of (O-5) LTC; I figured it was the highest rank I'd achieve, so why not enjoy it! I had already trained to become a Civil Affairs (CA) Officer and I started doing operations and planning in a Civil Affairs Brigade. The Civil Affairs branch is a hybrid creature. Prior to 9/11, all CA units were in the reserves. Essentially, CA operators work with civilian governments, organizations, and populations from national to local levels. As a reservist, we are essentially civilians in uniform — we understand how both work — and believe me, they work very differently!

Only the Army and Marines have CA operators; the Air Force relies on the Army to provide CA support to them and their overseas air bases. The Navy relies on CA operators from the Marines. When I trained as a CA officer, we had both soldiers and marines in our course.

I was lucky to work with the Air Force and write some of their CA plans for overseas air bases. I also participated in several joint exercises with them, including overseas exercises. I was always answering airmen's questions about strange Army customs when the Army units transitioned from the airbase to the Army forward area. As the only female "field" officer, I was constantly asked to advise the commander on "female" issues — boy that never got old in my twenty-seven-plus years. I'll let you in on a closely guarded secret: I never once asked a man for help with "male" issues!

My major deployment as a LTC was for peace-keeping in Bosnia as a result of the Dayton Peace Accords (signed December 15, 1995). I was stationed in Sarajevo as the Deputy J3 for the Combined Joint Civil Military Task Force (CJCMTF) and did operations for nine months. We had close to thirty nations working in our small Task Force. We worked in a building called "The Residency" that was once one of Marshall Tito's homes and we lived in a building called "The Parliament." The Parliament was steps away from the spot where Archduke Ferdinand and his pregnant wife, Sophie, were assassinated in 1914 by an anarchist, touching off WWI. They brought the Duke and his wife to the Parliament building, where they both died.

Sarajevo was once a beautiful city with a mixture of Ottoman ornate buildings and Soviet-era concrete-block buildings. The country was torn apart during its bloody civil war after Tito died and the international community was attempting to help Bosnia put together a three-party government. The three parties were in reality three ethnic/religious groups. I did a fair amount of traveling while in Bosnia; I went to Italy for planning and to Germany to spend a week with my family. The rank of 05 wears a silver oak leaf.

Commander's Flag, 48" x 50".
Designed and machine-pieced by Renelda Peldunas-
Harter; quilted by Carolyn Perry Goins.

Commander's Flag

LEVEL: Intermediate

FINISHED QUILT: 54" x 60"

FINISHED BLOCK: 12" x 12"

MATERIALS

(Yardage based on 44"-wide fabric)

- 2 yd. light blue (color 1) for block and border
- 2-1/2 yd. dark blue (color 2) for block and border
- 1 yd. medium yellow (color 3) for block

- Creative Grids™ Non-Slip 15° Triangle Ruler by Erin Underwood

CUTTING & SEWING

(All measurements include 1/4" seam)

Color 1 (light blue fabric): Cut 12 strips 2-1/2" x 44"

Color 2 (dark blue fabric): Cut 12 strips 3" x 44"

Color 3 (medium yellow fabric): Cut 12 strips 2-1/2" x 44"

1 Sew the strips together in the following order: color 1 (light) to color 2 (dark) to color 3 (medium) (**FIGURE 1**). Sew a total of 12 strip sets together in this sequence.

2 Press toward center (dark) strip. For consistency purposes, always have color 1 on the top of the unit.

FIGURE 1

1 Using a 15° ruler for a 15°-cut, cut the strip from top to bottom, right to left (**FIGURE 2**).

2 Measure 7" from cut corners, top and bottom, and mark (**FIGURE 3**).

3 Cut between the two marks (**FIGURE 4**).

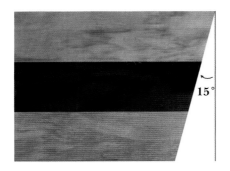

FIGURE 2

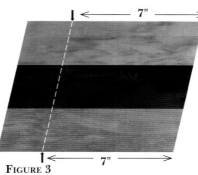
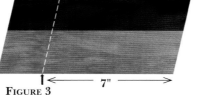

FIGURE 3

FIGURE 4

4 Measure 1/4" down from left top center strip, mark and measure 1/4" up from bottom right center strip, mark (**FIGURE 5**).

5 Cut center strip between the two marks (**FIGURE 6**).

6 Line up colors 1 and 3 and sew together; press toward darker color (**FIGURE 7**).

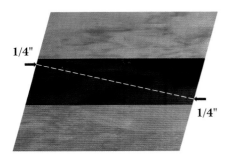

FIGURE 5

FIGURE 6

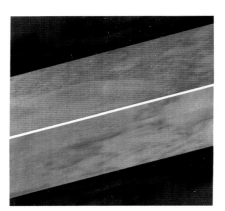

FIGURE 7

7 Using a 6-1/2" x 6-1/2" square ruler, square block.

8 Cut out 48 blocks.

9 Layout: Use caution as you lay out your squares! It is easy to reverse the squares, which throws off the pattern. Sew 4 blocks together to construct a 12-1/2" x 12-1/2" block, for a total of 12 blocks (**FIGURE 8**).

10 Square using a 12-1/2" x 12-1/2" square.

FIGURE 8

ASSEMBLE THE QUILT TOP

*Refer to the quilt assembly diagram to layout the 12-1/2" x 12-1/2" square blocks, 3 blocks across, 4 blocks down (**FIGURE 9**).*

FIGURE 9

BORDERS & BINDING

1 Before cutting and working on the borders, refer to Chapter 1, Finishing Phase, Squaring a quilt #2 and Borders #3.

2 Square your quilt and then measure and cut your borders, 2 opposite sides at a time.

3 Because of all the bias edges, the measurements can be off as much as 1/2". Accurate cutting of the inner border and plenty of pinning the border onto the quilt will ensure proper sizing.

4 Inner border: Measure along short side and cut 2 strips in color 1 (light blue fabric) 3" x 36-1/2" and 2 strips for long sides 3" x 53-1/4".

5 Outer border: Cut 2 strips of color 2 for short side 3-1/2" x 41-3/4" and 2 strips for long sides 3-1/2" x 59-1/2".

6 Cut binding 2-1/4" x 190".

Commander's Flag Gallery

Ann Marie Chaney's quilt *Corps of Engineers* takes the red and white (Engineer branch colors) and combines them with blue to create this stunning quilt. This 60" x 82" quilt is machine-pieced and machine-quilted by Ann; she selected this pattern for a number of reasons, primarily because she is a Lieutenant Colonel in the Army Reserves and wanted to do the O-5 quilt. However, she wanted to do the quilt in the colors of her branch — Corps of Engineer — and rearranged some of the colors: red is her "dark," blue is her "light," and the white is her "medium" color. Notice the four cornerstones of this quilt — engineer castles. This was Ann's way to make sure you know an engineer constructed this quilt!

Corps of Engineers, 60" x 82".
Machine-pieced and quilted by Ann Marie Chaney.

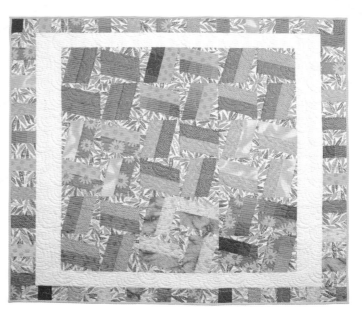

Fiesta!, 45" x 51".
Machine-pieced by Didi Salvatierra,
and machine-quilted by Peggy Graff.

Didi Salvatierra was on a mission to use a kid-friendly fabric bundle to give this 45" x 51" quilt a distinctly *Fiesta!* flavor. The quilt is machine-pieced by Didi and machine-quilted by Peggy Graff. Didi is an award-winning quilter and fiber artist. To see more of her traditional and art quilts, visit her website at www. didiquilts.com.

Chapter Seven

COLONEL'S STARS (O-6)

I was having way too much fun as a LTC! I did a lot of planning, coordinating, and exercises with the Air Force. I was sent back to Egypt for the same exercise I had participated in as a Captain. This time, I did not bother to brush up my language skills, although I did spend a great deal of time checking out civilian venues in anticipation of airmen- and soldier-sponsored visits to some of the major tourist sites. I stopped off in Rota, Spain, on my return from the exercise and spent too little time there. My two young sons were finally old enough that they didn't miss mom too much, so I spent more time traveling as I ventured to strange and exotic locations to conduct planning and operations — and then the unthinkable happened.

I was picked up for full Colonel (COL). The grade of O-6 is a colonel in the Army, Marines, and Air Force and a captain (CAPT) in the Navy and Coast Guard. Inter-service ranks can be tricky, with the army/ marine/air forces "Captain" being an O-3 and the navy/coast guard "Captain" being an O-6. As an O-3 Captain, I worked for a Navy O-6 Captain and it was always extremely difficult for him to address me as "Captain Peldunas"! My brother warned me that he would address me as "Miss" Peldunas, but if he ever did, he only did it once.

At my promotion ceremony, my two sons did the honor of pinning on my Colonel's eagles as my husband, mother, two of my three brothers, and scores of family and friends looked on. During comments (no matter what anyone tells you, being promoted to full colonel entitles one to make a speech!), I remember telling our two boys that as proud as I was to accomplish such a milestone, I would be much prouder to pin eagles on their Boy Scout uniforms. Two years later both boys received their Boy Scout Eagle Awards and it was a very proud mom and dad who pinned the awards to their Boy Scout uniforms.

I had only been a colonel for a little while before my unit started to mobilize for the invasion of Iraq. I mobilized with my unit, but health reasons prevented me from deploying with them then or at a subsequent time. With the unit deployed, the "Family Support" team (spouses of the unit members) did a fantastic job keeping everyone in the loop and assisting when needed. Our operation NCO's wife helped my son, Kevin, with his Eagle Scout project. Kevin's project was to supervise the making of 125 "care packages" for the unit, and the Family Support team came up with the money so he could mail the packages.

I retired not long after the unit returned from deployment. All-in-all, I had spent seven years on active duty and over twenty years as a reservist. My final promotion came as I was promoted to "civilian/ veteran." Best promotion ever!

As a civilian, I decided to make a series of quilts on the topic I knew the most about — the military — and, thus, was born the first book in the ongoing series "Making Quilts to Honor Those Who Serve." I started with the officer ranks since they were something I knew about.

The *Colonel's Star* quilt was the first quilt I designed for this series. It is comprised of askew star blocks signifying the general's/admiral's stars that are ready and waiting for the colonel/captain to reach out and grasp onto! The rank of 06 wears an eagle.

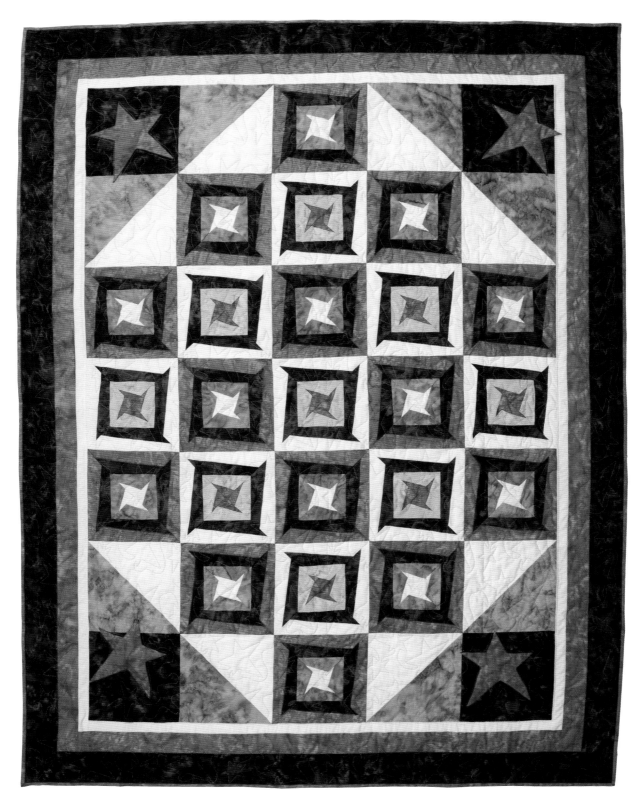

Colonel's Star, 55" x 42".
Designed and pieced by Renelda Peldunas-Harter;
quilted by Carolyn Perry Goins.

Colonel's Stars

LEVEL: Intermediate

FINISHED QUILT: 55" x 72"

FINISHED BLOCK: 8-1/2" x 8-1/2"

MATERIALS

(Yardage based on 44"-wide fabric)

- 1-3/4 yd. red for blocks and middle border
- 1-1/2 yd. white for blocks and inner border
- 3/4 yd. light blue for blocks

- 1 yd. medium blue for blocks
- 2-1/4 yd. dark blue for blocks and outer border
- Gridded Plastic Template Sheet, 12" x 18"

CUTTING & SEWING

(All measurements include 1/4" seam)

1 Cut for Red Block:

Red fabric (color 1): Cut 12 strips of 2-1/4" x 44"

Dark blue (color 2): Cut 12 strips of 2" x 44"

Medium blue (color 3): Cut 6 strips of 2-3/4" x 44"

White (color 4): Cut 6 strips of 1-1/2" x 44"

2 Cut for White Block:

White fabric (color 1): Cut 8 strips of 2-1/4" x 44"

Dark blue (color 2): Cut 8 strips of 2" x 44"

Light blue (color 3): Cut 4 strips of 2-3/4" x 44"

Red (color 4): Cut 4 strips of 1-1/2" x 44"

3 Sew for Red Block:

A. Sew the 12 red strips (color 1) to the 12 dark blue strips (color 2) (**FIGURE 1**), set aside.

B. Sew the 6 medium blue (color 3) to the 6 white strips (color 4) (**FIGURE 2**), set aside.

4 Sew for White Block:

A. Sew the 8 white (color 1) to the 8 dark blue strips (color 2) (**FIGURE 3**), set aside.

B. Sew the 4 light blue (color 3) to the 4 red strips (color 4) (**FIGURE 4**), set aside.

5. Blue and white half-square triangle block: Cut out 4 each 9-3/4" x 9-3/4" white and light blue squares. Set aside.

6. Cut out 4 dark blue squares, 9" x 9" each. Set aside.

FIGURE 1

FIGURE 3

FIGURE 2

FIGURE 4

BLOCK CONSTRUCTION

1. The *Colonel's Star* quilt has 35 blocks, comprised of 14 Red Star blocks, 9 White Star blocks, 8 Blue and White half-square triangle blocks, and 4 Dark Blue blocks.

2. Using the plastic template sheet, cut out both templates (**FIGURES 5 AND 6**). The templates appear at the end of the chapter (attachment 1); the 1/4" seam allowance has been added. Refer to the figures and cut out the notches where indicated.

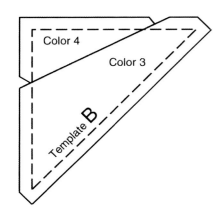

FIGURE 5

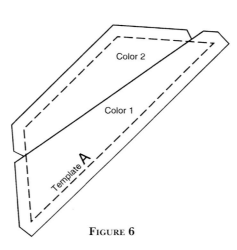

FIGURE 6

3 Start with the fabric for the Red Block. Place **Template A** on top of the color 1 & 2 strip. The line goes over the seam line and through the notches (**FIGURE 7**). Cut a total of 56 for the Red Block.

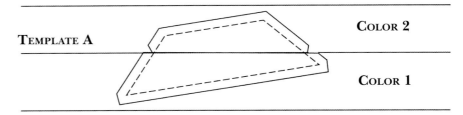

TEMPLATE A

COLOR 2

COLOR 1

FIGURE 7

4 Place **Template B** on top of the color 3 & 4 strip. The line goes over the seam line and through the notches (**FIGURE 8**). Cut a total of 56 for the Red Block.

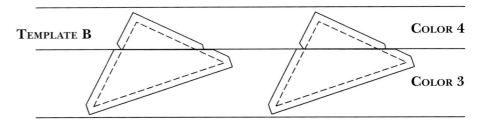

TEMPLATE B

COLOR 4

COLOR 3

FIGURE 8

5 Sew Template A piece to Template B piece, thus creating a pyramid shape (**FIGURE 9**) for a total of 56 pyramids.

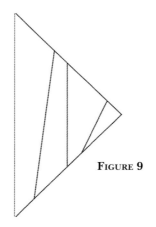

FIGURE 9

6 Pressing: Press towards what will be the center. Use starch or light body sizing to stabilize your fabrics throughout.

7 Each block is comprised of four pyramids (**FIGURES 10A AND 10B**). Sew together in units of 2. Sew the units of two together to complete construction of the block. There will be 14 Red blocks. Square blocks to 9" x 9".

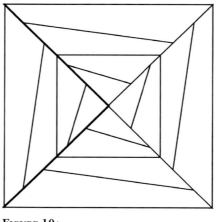

FIGURE 10A

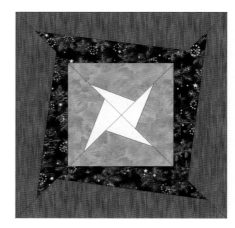

FIGURE 10B

8 Repeat steps 3-7 with the fabric for the White Block. Cut a total of 36 pyramids for the White Block. There will be 9 complete White blocks.

9 For construction of the blue and white half-square triangle squares, place one white square, right side up, and one light blue square, right side down, facing the white square. With right sides facing together, fold in half, corner to corner, and press (**FIGURE 11**).

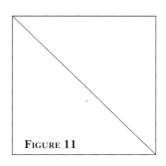

FIGURE 11

10 Sew 1/4" from press line on both sides of press line (**FIGURE 12**). With a rotary cutter, cut on the press line, separate both halves, open fabric, and press (**FIGURE 13**). Square block to 9" x 9".

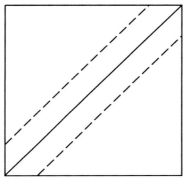

FIGURE 12

FIGURE 13

ASSEMBLE THE QUILT TOP

FIGURE 14

1 Refer to the quilt assembly diagram (**FIGURE 14**) to lay out blocks. Sew the blocks in rows across the quilt and then sew the rows together.

2 Appliqué corner stars: Refer to Chapter 1, Construction Phase, #5 for instructions on appliquéing the star onto the quilt. The appliqué for the star is attached at the end of the chapter (attachment 2).

3 Position and pin the star mostly on the dark blue corner fabric. Appliqué the star onto the dark blue square using the needle turn method (see Chapter 1, Applique Tips).

1 Before cutting and working on the borders, first see Chapter 1, Finishing Phase, Squaring a quilt #2 and Borders #3.

2 Square your quilt and then measure and cut your borders, 2 opposite sides at a time.

3 Because of all the bias edges, the measurements can be off as much as 1/2". Accurate cutting of the inner border and plenty of pinning the border onto the quilt will ensure proper sizing.

4 Inner border (white): cut two 43" x 1-1/2"; sew onto the quilt and cut two 62" x 1-1/2"; sew on the quilt and press.

5 Middle border (red): cut two 45" x 2-1/2"; sew onto the quilt and cut two 66" x 2-1/2"; sew onto quilt and press.

6 Outer border (dark blue): cut two 49" x 3-1/2"; sew onto the quilt and cut two 72" x 3-1/2"; sew onto quilt and press.

7 Cut binding to 2-1/2" x 280".

Colonel's Star Gallery

Cindy Sisler Simms fell in love with the Colonel's Star — so she created three distinct and unique quilts around the block!

This quilt, called *Windblown Stars*, has Cindy drafting the block in five different sizes. When she saw the original block, the idea of blowing stars popped into her head, but it took working on the next two quilts before she could draft the different sizes for this quilt. This quilt reminds Cindy of a star exploding and twirling around in the wind.

Windblown Stars, 33" x 33". Machine-pieced and quilted by Cindy Sisler Simms.

Night Stars, 41" x 41".
Machine-pieced and quilted by Cindy Sisler Simms.

Cindy's second "Star" quilt is this 41" x 41" quilt called *Night Stars*. This quilt creates movement and the sense of one star exploding into many stars by the use of colors and block placement. Cindy enlisted into the Women's Army Corps (WACs) after graduating from high school. She met her husband, who was also on active duty, in the military. Cindy got out of the Army, but made many moves, as her husband spent 27 years on active duty. Cindy comes from a long and proud military family tradition: World War II and Korea saw her father, her uncles, and her husband's father all serving.

The third of Cindy's "Star" quilts is the 42" x 42" beauty called *Sea Gems*. The colors and setting reminded her of a starfish, but she still felt like something was missing. It turned out to be a guild auction fabric with dolphins that pulled the ocean-like setting all together. In all three of Cindy's quilts, she uses both cottons and cotton/polyester blends to create the effect she is after. All the quilts were machine-pieced and machine-quilted by Cindy.

Sea Gems, 42" x 42".
Machine-pieced and quilted by Cindy Sisler Simms.

The author's *Christmas Star* is a 36" x 36" wall-hanging with semi-traditional Christmas colors. This was my idea to try something different and to see what colors I could make "pop." The light burnt orange draws the eye whereas the dark green fades into the background. This is an easy quilt for practicing the "Star" blocks.

Christmas Star, 36" x 36".
Machine-pieced and quilted by Renelda Peldunas-Harter.

Corner star for *Colonel's Star* quilt. A 1/4" seam has NOT been added to this template. If using the needle turn method to appliqué this star to the quilt, then add 1/4".

Template A and **Template B** for the *Colonel's Star* quilt. The 1/4" seam allowance HAS been added to this template. Be sure to "notch" the template at the appropriate places in order to line up the seam between your two fabrics (see accompanying pattern draft).

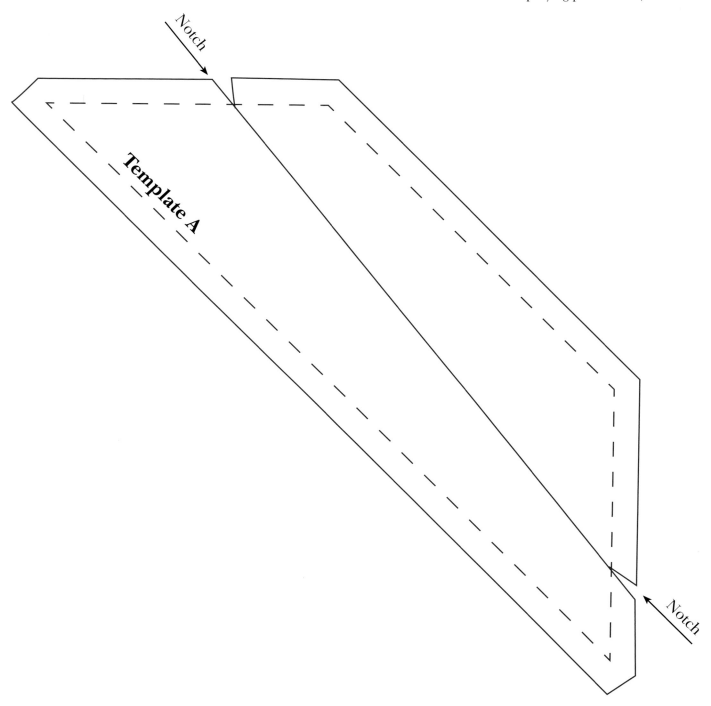

Notch

Template A

Notch

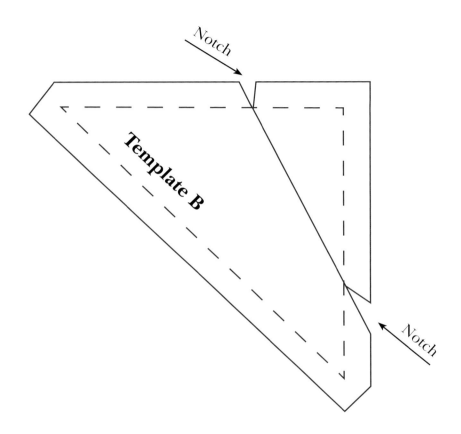

Notch

Template B

Notch

Chapter Eight

MILITARY OFFICER RANKS

Officer Ranks: Commissioned officer ranks are designated as "Officer" or "O" and the number.

O-1: Army, Marines, and Air Force: **2ⁿᵈ Lieutenant** (A-2LT, M-2ⁿᵈ Lt, AF-2ⁿᵈ Lt); Navy and Coast Guard: **Ensign** (ENS)

O-2: Army, Marines, and Air Force: **1ˢᵗ Lieutenant** (A-1LT, M-1ˢᵗ Lt, AF-1ˢᵗ Lt); Navy and Coast Guard: **Lieutenant, Junior Grade** (LTJG)

O-3: Army, Marines, and Air Force: **Captain** (A-CPT, M-Capt, AF-Capt); Navy and Coast Guard: **Lieutenant** (LT)

O-4: Army, Marines, and Air Force: **Major** (A-MAJ, M-Maj, AF-Maj); Navy and Coast Guard: **Lieutenant Commander** (LCDR)

O-5: Army, Marines, and Air Force: **Lieutenant Colonel** (A-LTC, M-LtCol, AF-Lt Col); Navy and Coast Guard: **Commander** (CDR)

O-6: Army, Marines, and Air Force: **Colonel** (A-COL, M-Col, AF-Col); Navy and Coast Guard: **Captain** (CAPT)

This is the story of the significance behind the insignia as told to me (by whom is lost in time) when I was a young lieutenant. The story goes something like this:

The element gold (Au) is the most precious metal and it is buried deep in the ground, the deepest of the precious metals. One must work hard and long to possess it (4 years of college). A gold bar is the hardest medal to get.

The element silver (Ag) is the second most precious metal; it lies above gold in the earth. The silver bar comes next.

Two silver bars are twice as precious as one silver bar. You have proven your worth by digging the precious metal out of the ground and you have earned the honor to move on to become a "field" officer.

Gold oak leaves come from the bottom of the mighty oak tree. The oak stands solid and true.

Silver oak leaves come from the top of the mighty oak. You are leaving the earth and reaching for the sky.

The eagle soars above the earth and trees, free of the confines of the earth, soaring as high as she can go.

The stars reside above both the earth and the soaring eagle.

RESOURCES

SUPPLIERS/ INFORMATION

HOFFMAN CALIFORNIA FABRICS
www.hoffmanfabrics.com
800-547-0100

WINDHAM FABRICS
www.windhamfabrics.com
866-842-7631

STEAM-A-SEAM 2®
www.warmcompany.com
800-234-9276

SULKY®
www.sulky.com
800-874-4115

Creative Grids®
www.creativegridsusa.com

WEB INFORMATION

- To find out more information about the QUILTS OF VALOR FOUNDATION, please visit their website at www.QOVF.org.

- You can follow RENELDA PELDUNAS-HARTER on her blog at www.QuiltedCora.blogspot.com.

Renelda will be working on her next book in the series "Making Quilts to Honor Those Who Serve" with quilts for the enlisted ranks starting in 2016. If you are interested in working on one of the seven quilts for that book, please email her at r.peldunas@comcast.net.